ZERO TO ZILLIONS
BY
ORU RUSSELL

DEDICATION

This book is dedicated to all those who believed in me

To dad and mom for your un-ending love and support

To Obi Emanuel for your mentoring

To Oru, Orubau and Kokenam for being more than family

And to every great mind out there yet to discover their talents

ACKNOWLEDGEMENTS

Growing up I was surrounded with all kinds of books; dictionaries, Literature, History etc., sometimes I had too much to read. At every point in time I had access to the kind of books I wanted to read. As far back as I could remember I have always wanted to be a writer and as a growing adult, writing proposals and business plans was a hobby rather than a need. Been exposed to books at such young age has been one key reason why you are reading Zero to Zillions.

I owe a tremendous debt of gratitude to the many people who helped make this book a reality.

First and foremost I want to thank the heavenly creator and Almighty God for his infinite mercy, grace and wisdom; to him alone I owe my praise.

To my biggest inspiration, President Goodluck Jonathan, every day you give me a reason to work harder, being the first president to have come from the South South region of Nigeria, you have given a lot of us believe that anything is possible if you work hard. Your rise to the biggest position as GCFR in Nigeria is a proof that hard work, focus, honesty and diligence pay. I am proud to say that your story is one of the essence of Zero to Zillions.

To my dear Bayelsa State; for always encouraging youths with training programmes to reduce restiveness and alleviate poverty.

To my parents Mr. and Mrs. Oru, I owe my biggest gratitude to you both for your unreserved love and care. A zillion thanks to the best dad in the world who has made this book a possibility by giving me unrivaled guidance and support.

To Mr. and Mrs. Obi Emmanuel my second parents, one man who has done much more than words can say. I hope that one day I would be able to make him proud and repay all his kind deeds and gestures.

To Mr. and Mrs. Giwa Amu, for the wonderful experience in France (Paris) and Belgium, whatever you do, I pray God rewards you.

In the course of my business as a web designer and ICT consultant, I have met some amazing and inspiring people; To Barr. Esueme Dan Kikile, Engr. Dio Wenapere, Mr. Barry Peremongu, Capt. Ken Ateb, Dr. Princewill Igbagara, Hon. Tonye Isenah, Mr. Egba Livingstone, Hon. Ogbomade, Barr. Dandy, Mr. Timi Amah, Mr. Jonathan David and Mr. Ambrose Odibo. I am grateful to have worked with each and every one of you sirs.

To my lecturers at Gates Intense Securities and Network Solution Training in Mumbai, India; Mrs. Varsha Shety, Mr. Muralhedeen, Mr. Binduraj, Sarika, Pretha and Varsha. I am eternally grateful.

To my Theatre Arts Lecturers in Niger Delta University, Prof. S.N.A Agoro, Prof. Bell Gam, Dr. Ken Eni, Dr. Ben Binebai, Dr. Abraye, Dr. Christine Odi and Mr. Rudolph Kan Sese. You all make learning a hobby. Every day I learn new things from you. You are all simply the best lecturers any student can have.

To my lovely sibling; Oru, Kokenam, Imorobebh, Orubau, Daniel, Favour, Eyal. The best family I could ever have.

Launching this book without these five names would have been impossible. This five fantastic, innovative, creative and project based team have worked effortlessly with me to make this a possibility. To Lanny Clement, Ipoweido Jackson, Diri Priye, Ebi Kutu and Kind Dickson I am grateful.

To my friends, Temerigha Happiness, Ladebi Simeni, Tonye Timi, Atsemude Phebe, Atsemude Joshua, Omoruyi Efosa, Anesah Dalayefa, Iyabi Janet, Bokiri Justina, Nwoargu Amina, Dick-Agbe Tarilate Whitney, Daumiebi Jackson, Oweifie Kelvin, Ugo Fabian, Akusu Roy, Arabina Ebizimo, Waribo Christiana, Waribo Mabel, Funkeyi Eduke and Okwodu Jeffrey, thanks for always being there for me.

And finally to every individual who has affected me positively in one way or the other, my friends during my French sojourns and my friends in France, India, Belgium, South Africa, Togo, Cameroun and Ghana.

I say thank you and God bless.

CHAPTER ONE

DEVELOPING YOUR HOBBY

How Mark Zuckerberg made billions from his dormitory

> "Today is life-the only life you are sure of. Make the most of today. Get interested in something. Shake yourself awake. Develop a hobby. Let the winds of enthusiasm sweep through you. Live today with gusto".
> Dale Carnegie

The year was 1984; the year Apple Macintosh was introduced, sadly Indian Prime minister Indira Gandhi was assassinated by her two Sikh security guards. Same year precisely on the 31st of October, five months before the death of Indira Gandhi, the future of Social media had its first breath. An American computer programmer and Internet entrepreneur was born, named Mark Zuckerberg.

The year 2012, and Mark Zuckerberg is the Chief Executive officer of Facebook Inc.; the biggest social networking website ever known to man.

Born and raised in New York State, Zuckerberg took up writing software programmes as a hobby in middle school; tutored by his dad and at some point by a programmer who described Zuckerberg as a prodigy at age thirteen, in middle school.

According to the writer Jose Antonio Vargas, "some kids played computer games. Mark created them." Zuckerberg himself recalls this period: his friends would draw up games and he would create them using his programming skills.

In 2003 Facemash was designed, a website that let students select the best looking person from a choice of photos. A website he designed for fun, some days later it was closed by school authority.

In February 4, 2004 Facebook was launched by Zuckerberg from his Harvard dormitory. It was later redesigned with help from his college roommates and fellow Harvard University students, Eduardo Saverin, Andrew McCollum, Dustin Moskovitz and Chris Hughes; a social network service was launched. The new service would later change the way business is done, will change communication forever and make life easier and learning less boring; a service that has gained over a billion users as at the time of publication of this book.

In the Year 2007, what started as a hobby was turning into a huge business and some major corporations were making offers to buy out Facebook.

Zuckerberg turned them down explaining the reason saying;

- ✓ Not because of the amount of money, for me and my colleagues, the most important thing is that we create an open information flow for people, having media corporations owned by conglomerates is just not an attractive idea to me, the thing I really care about is the mission, making the world open.

- ✓ **Nothing is more important than your mission**

Explaining further he says "the need to open up and connect is what makes us humans, what brings us together, and what brings meaning to our lives".

- ✓ **Your mission should add meaning to your life and that of others.**

At the time of publication of this book, Facebook has over four thousand employees and offices in fifteen countries all over the world.

Today Facebook is used by everyone; from churches to politicians, athletes to celebrities, businesses to individuals, all kinds of people use Facebook for different reasons but still the mission is reflected in each of these reasons. What makes Facebook so spectacular and appealing to web users is its simplicity, the fact that you can easily communicate and connect without much work.

At Facebook they build tools to help people and business connect and share with people they want to. Mark Zuckerberg was quoted as saying "The thing that we are trying to do at Facebook, is just to help people connect and communicate efficiently"

Your mission should be aimed at achieving your vision

Turn your hobby into a profession.

I define a hobby as regular activity or interest that is undertaken for pleasure, mostly done during one's leisure time. Examples of hobbies include sports, artistic drawing, painting, cooking, singing etc. A profession according to dictionary.com is a paid occupation that involves prolonged training or formal training. Examples of professionals are bankers, computer programmers, footballers, musicians, models, doctors, lawyers, engineers etc.

A professional is a person who is paid to undertake a specialized set of tasks and to complete them for a fee. Basically the difference between both is the fee, and the fact that the professional is known for the particular field in which he or she does.

Qualities of a good professional

- Expert and specialized knowledge in field which one is practicing professionally.

Good communication skills in relation to the specified job, high quality work which leaves both clients and customers satisfied.

A very good standard of professional ethics, behavior and work activities while doing his or her job.

Hobby, Interest and Profession

Do you have a hobby? Something that makes you happy doing; something that interests you, do you love painting, dancing, marketing or photography? Have you ever thought of spending more time in developing that hobby?

The problem with choosing a profession most times is that, people consider the job security in terms of how much it pays and they never think of how much they like doing the job or how good they can do the job. Are we not supposed to choose a profession that brings out the best in our abilities because it is something we would most probably do for the rest of our lives? Why then do so many people not even think about their hobbies when a hobby could in fact be a profession in waiting?

- **Every profession has requirements and your leverage is your hobby, it is easier doing what you love.**

Hobbies are the things you choose to do, activities that you are probably good at and enjoy doing, and these personal expressions "will give us unedited clues as to our real desires and interests," says Joyce K. Reynolds, an expert business coach.

Also this is what Career coach Phyllis Mufson has to say about hobbies, interest and profession. "A hobby you really enjoy can be an important part of choosing a career because your hobby is a window into what you love and value and do most naturally, which are all important components of a career where you will flourish."

Do not wait for someone to hire you:

Yes you do not need someone to hire you. Employ yourself just like Zuckerberg, you can provide yourself a job; the job of making a profession out of your hobby, besides that, you are good at your hobby for a reason, so go ahead and continuously practice it until it becomes a profession.

Improve on your hobby:

The only shot you have at turning your hobby into a profession is improving your hobby. If you do not improve then you would probably end with it as a hobby. Constant practice should help you achieve that. The more you learn the more you improve, they say practice makes perfection. Remember the greatest footballer of our generation once played orange as football, the Argentine genius Lionel Messi who has broken all the available football records. Messi was never this good; ten years ago he was just an ordinary footballer like the rest. It was his determination to get better each day, his constant practices, his obsession for perfection. Knowing the odds will go a long way for you. Always know this until you are a professional, you are not good enough and even when you are, you are still not good enough. So the only way to show the world that you are good enough is through hard work.

Do your homework:

Sometimes the only reason it gets difficult turning a hobby into a profession is because you are not well informed, you do not know how to showcase your hobby on the big stage. You have not done your research appropriately or you have not done it at all. The difference between you and the professional is more training and that is something you can attain by yourself. Why not research and know all there is to know about your future profession. It gets easier when you know what you are doing. Doing your homework is giving yourself more advantage, putting yourself in the right position to succeed.

Teach others your hobby:

Have you ever asked any teacher why they continue to teach even though the salary does not match their output? Well I have asked many and they all gave me the same reason. "I love teaching, it is my hobby" was a response by one of the numerous teachers I asked. Explaining further they believe that the more you teach, the more you learn. It is a cycle that never ends. You can learn from teachers today.

Speak and Write about your hobby:

Another way of attaining success with your hobby is through writing and speaking about it. Write it, share it and teach it. There is a need for you to create an avenue for people to learn what you know.

It is time to leave your dormitory

In this context, leaving your dormitory means defeating self-doubt and starting something.

- ✓ **The right time is now**

Ever wondered how many questions Mark Zuckerberg must have asked himself before venturing into Facebook? Ever wondered how many people must have advised him against it? Self-doubt is a killer of dreams; you have to defeat it to achieve success.

Not only was his timing right, but the product was right too. Most times people kill their dreams by staying too long in the dormitory. A lot of people have killed their dreams by spending too much action time on planning, some are scared to try because they think the world will not appreciate them, others are waiting on fate to do something.

Surely the time to leave your dormitory is now. Leaving your dormitory is not about dropping out of school or running away from your home, it is about becoming a professional and it is taking the decision to turn your hobby into a profession.

- ✓ **It is safer to start now**

There will always be reasons why you cannot start now. Reasons why you should delay your project, reasons like; I Just started school, I just got married, I just finished school and the 'I do not have money to start a bussiness' syndrome.

So what?

These are mere excuses that will kill your dreams the moment you pay attention to them.

So you just got married? Good, start something now for your kids.

You just got admission; you should know that going to school is not enough, school does not guarantee you a secured financial life.

Finishing school is not an excuse either, the lessons you have learnt in school will even help you in the pursuit of your hobby as a profession. You have studied enough and it is time to apply what you have learnt in school.

And for those who have issues with capital, it is all about 'packaging' package your ideas and concepts and sell to individuals, companies and government parastatals. Your job is making the ideas and concepts unique and you can be sure of good patronage.

The time is now because you know what to do; everything you need is now within your reach. Remember that starting now means testing your capabilities and unleashing your potentials.

Times have changed

Before now all you needed was go to school, graduate and look for a safe and secure job, work for years and retire so that the government or your company takes care of you for the rest of your life. In today's world no job is safe. Technological advancement means that a single click of the computer can do anything; thousands of jobs are lost every day. Secondly it is never safe to depend on the government or a company for retirement benefits. What if they fail you? What if they fail us? There could be only one answer if this happens. Our last years will be hell on earth, no money to feed and none for medical bills.

Even been a first-class graduate is not a guarantee for a job, too many over qualified graduates are applying for the same job so your chances are just as good as any of the others. So why not create jobs rather than look for one.

Why not be the guy who fires rather than been the guy who gets fired?

If Bill gates and Steve Jobs had waited for a job after school, the over three hundred thousand employees of Apple and Microsoft would have been unemployed. It is time to stop think, it is time to act. A lot of people have died with ideas that could have changed the world.

Anyone can do anything if he puts enough effort, always remember that great athletes are trained and not born. That is the belief of a champion.

You may not be good at any hobby today, but after reading this I recommend you to learn one and make a difference in your life.

Baking, Basket Weaving, Computer programming, Cooking, Coloring, Creative writing, Dance, Drawing, Home automation, Jewelry making, Knitting, Musical instruments, Painting, Sculpting Sewing, Singing, Woodworking, Writing, Cycling, Driving, Gardening, Photography, Swimming, Antiquing., Art collecting, Bowling, Boxing, Chess, Billiards, Darts, Dancing, Gymnastics, Martial arts, Handball, Badminton, Baseball, Basketball, Climbing, Cricket, Cycling, Fishing, Swimming, Tennis, Volleyball, Reading, Aquarium making

- ✓ **Learn a hobby today and never look back**

CHAPTER TWO

STARTING SMALL
Growing bigger and getting there with the right business

> "The first step towards getting somewhere is to decide that you are not going to stay where you are."
> Morgan, John Pierpont

When trying to start a business most times we often find ourselves asking so many unnecessary questions and not getting the right answers, when it comes to business it is better to do it the Nike way "Just do it" before starting a business it is good to do a lot of research, read books and magazines, surf the net to get detailed information on the business you are about to venture into, analyze your business, know your target market and how to penetrate. These processes would help you to get more information on how to go about it.

Business is not for lazy people

Getting your business off the ground requires a lot of focus, determination, hard work, time and sweat.
Once you are aware of all these, the possibility of business failure will reduce. Here is a list of businesses that you can start on a
 Zero budget, they are businesses with an available market and their success chances are very high.

Web Design Service

Have you ever felt like the world is slowly moving past you, you do not seem to know the latest lingua anymore and most of the information in your head is not to up to date. If you feel this way then it is because you have not been using the internet. There are over a billion web users and web pages and statistics show over 300 million people use the internet daily. The addiction of the web cannot be under emphasized, the internet is now a global phenomenon and everyone who wants to remain useful to his society must know how to take advantage of the web.

✓ **Each and every web page on the net is designed by a web designer**

This is one business where you really do not need any money to start; all you need is to have is some formal training and a lot of practice to get started. This is one service that will surely get you up there in no time. Every business needs a website; all you need do is to be very good at it. Give your clients first class designs and logos and expect as many referrals in no time. You can make anywhere from a hundred thousand naira to millions in just your first year in business.

Just by making simple database and graphic sites for business and individuals, for the clients that already have a website, they will need someone to keep it up to date with fresh content.

Start a Blog

Are you an expert in a particular area? Like science, relationships, arts or even making money; if you can get people to read your opinions then you are in big business.

Blogging as a business is all about creating outstanding content. The better your content, the more people would want you. The more people come to your blog/site, the more opportunity there is for you to make a name and business out of it.

Blogs are a great way to attract and communicate with customers, improve your search engine optimization (SEO), and yes, make good money. If you do it right.

Chose a niche you are passionate about and write about it daily, there are thousands of affiliate programs and websites ready to pay you when people click through from your blog to their sites and make a purchase. Expect to spend money on a domain name, hosting, a good blog template, and maybe some online marketing.

Social Media Consulting

Ever wondered how Mark Zuckerberg makes money from Facebook? Well, most of it comes from ads on the right hand column of your Facebook page. The designer websites and bank sites you click when on Facebook, they are basically the reason he is a billionaire.

And do you also know you can make millions just being on Facebook and twitter? Did you also know this stuff is big business? Well it absolutely is.

There are entire consulting firms dedicated to helping their clients maximize their social media efforts, and some of them probably do not have as much experience at it as you do.

Step one is to find out all you can about using social media for business. Next, decide what services you will offer and if you will specialize in a particular area. Facebook fan pages, for instance. Then get out there on social media and make it known that you are available as a consultant.

It is time to use your social media skills to attract thousands of followers to businesses and increase their click traffic while you make a business and good money for yourself.

Now you have a business. There is no question that social media has become a necessary part of every marketer's playbook, but not many know how to do it right.

That is where you will step in and make a fortune showing them the way. Lots of politicians, churches and businesses are waiting for you to make your move and contact them.

Custom Engraving

If you can trace, then this business is for you. Basically a home business that is both enjoyable and profitable. You can make a wonderful income and create satisfying business shirts, caps, Wood, stone, glass, and lots more. Come up with witty slogans and sell your T-shirts, caps and etc. You should be prepared to have too many jobs at a time because the demand for custom engravings is very high.

As you may know, the demand for personalized custom engraving is rapidly and steadily growing. And while custom engraving was formerly limited to extremely talented creative artists and craftsmen, you can work hard and get an engraving system that enables you to produce elaborately engraved custom designs that match the skills of the finest engravers.

More and more people are buying personalized engraving today, both for decorative purposes and to protect valuables with identification. They add names, initials, company logos, custom designs and more to all kinds of items: glassware and gifts, trophies and awards, golf clubs, clocks, cameras, and ceramics, tools and toys - the list goes on! When you begin marketing your engraving services, you will probably choose a target market, and select areas to specialize in as your personal style develops. As you grow, you may expand into new, diverse markets

Event Planning

If you are the person your friends come to when they need help planning their wedding and social functions, book launches and birthday parties. You are the one who puts everything together for an event to hold successfully.

If you are very organized and like paying attention to detail, then this is for you.

Event Planning is a business that depends on your knowledge and ability to connect with people, more than anything that costs you money.

If you are super organized, able to perform well under pressure, and enjoy pleasing picky clients, this could be the business for you.

You are super detail oriented and able to juggle a million important tasks at the same time. You love planning every detail of an event and get great satisfaction out of seeing it come off without a hitch.

From weddings and family reunions to corporate functions and conventions, event planners are in demand just about everywhere.

Great event planners charge thousands of naira an hour for their services, and their clients pay for venues and equipment, so the overhead can be very low.

You will need to do a lot of networking, so getting some attractive, professional business cards printed would help.

The hours are long, and the work is not easy, but the rewards can be great.

Jewelry making

Jewelry Making is a business for those with a creative flare. It might take a little more to get started, both in money and know-how, but you do not need tons of training, and if you use materials like beads and silver rather than gold and diamonds, starting a jewelry business does not have to cost a lot.

To get started, you can learn most of what you need to know from Internet and books on the subject. Then it is a matter of practicing until you are good. If your stuff is attractive, you will find a market eager to snatch up your pieces, often for a premium price.

Home Delivery Service:

You can start your own business offering home delivery service by tying in with stores and home centers that do not already provide this service. People are pressed for time and the population is getting older. Consumers want goods delivered right to their doors.

The items you deliver could include groceries, hardware, food items etc. Canvass the neighborhood and ask store managers/owners if they could permit you to distribute business cards, flyers in their stores to drum up business. Perhaps they recommend you directly to their customers or hire you to perform the much-needed service directly.

Google AdSense

Do you already have a website, or are you thinking about building one? Whether it is a blog, an information site, or even a product site, many people make a living off their efforts with Google AdSense; basically, you are just going to place Google text ads on your site, for which Google will pay you. Of course there is a lot more to making a living at it, but again, anyone can do it, and Google provides some outstanding tools to help you along the way. If you want to learn more from someone who has done very well at it, check out Google Income: How anyone can build a highly profitable online business with Google.

Consultancy

If you know a lot about a particular subject, there are people willing to pay you for your expertise. Becoming a consultant is simply a matter of calling yourself one but being successful at consulting takes a lot of hard work and discipline.

What it usually does not take is a lot of money at least to start. You need a lot of networking to start this business; you will need some very professional business cards and an appropriate wardrobe for the job. Beyond that, a good website and some slick brochures will be necessary. More than anything else though, consultants are hired for who they are and what they know more so than their marketing materials, so you can get your first job or two without spending a dime.

CHAPTER THREE

RULES OF ZERO START UP

> "How dreadful... to be caught up in a game and have no idea of the rules" Caroline Stevermer

Rules are usually standards for doing a particular thing, rules define and constrain the way things ought to be done. Business rules are intended to assert business structure or to control and influence the behavior of the business. It can apply to people, processes, corporate and organizational setup.

There is no one rule that works for every one when it comes to business. Different rules work for different people; it all depends on the application of these rules. So if you are reading this and wondering if just following these rules would guarantee your success then I would say NO. You have to learn them, research about these rules and apply them in your chosen field.

✓ **The right application of rules will work for you**

Follow your passion.

> "What I know is, if you do work that you love, and work that fulfills you, the rest will come. And, I truly believe, that the reason I've been able to be so financially successful is because my focus has never, ever for one minute been money." **Oprah Winfrey**

So why do you want to start a business?

Sure you want to be your own boss, make lots of money, and leave your job that does not pay well.

Good reasons I must say but the truth is doing this would just be a way of running away from one job to another and as soon as you are not making enough money you would look for the nearest available flight to the next job.

You need to run towards a life that you do like.

If you look at successful entrepreneurs you would discover that it was never about the money. Successful entrepreneurs start businesses because they have a strong passion for it and want to make a powerful and lasting impact.

When you do meaningful work, you will earn more than money. What are you passionate about?

You can make money with any business idea if you are truly passionate about it and are providing real value to your customers.

The more value you provide, the more money you will make.

Find Your First Customer yourself

> "Of course I was underestimated. I was young, and this was a new industry. I just used it to my advantage. I had more energy and I didn't have any preconceived notions on how things should be. I just tried to learn the technology better than anyone else and find the best ways to help my customers."
> **Mark Cuban**

The most profitable way to start a business is by working with a customer who will pay you to solve a problem for them.

Most entrepreneurs do the exact opposite. They spend money and time trying to launch a product or service only to find that nobody wants to buy it.

Try as much as possible not to start your business until you have a paying customer. That way you are starting with money coming in right away.

Here's a quick example from my story:

I had an idea of creating a website that would give every business in my state a business page. A business directory website that meant even the smallest business in my state would be online. We designed it and were very proud of it. It was not until after the launch of the website, we started asking people questions and convincing customers to queue in that we realized they never needed what we were offering them.

We built it thinking they would love it but did not ask them first.

I hope you can learn from my mistake and not make the same one yourself!

Start talking to your potential customers. Get to know them and their challenges.

When you find people with a major pain and you have the ability to help them, you are ready to launch your business!

Until then, keep trying to find that product which would be relevant to your target market!

Charge more, provide more value

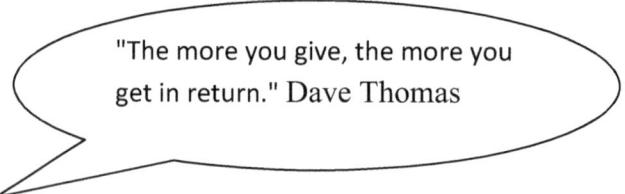

"The more you give, the more you get in return." Dave Thomas

We all want to make lots of money so much that sometimes we all forget that the customers who are paying for our services also work hard to make money, hence deserve quality products/services. Customers need to appreciate services more each day. To continuously woo clients we need to wow them each time they come, that means each day they work into your company you are providing them more value than the last time.

Want to make more money? Provide more value.

Want to beat out your competition? Provide more value than they do.

Want to make lots of money quickly? Provide lots of value quickly!

Providing more value does not mean you're discounting your prices. It means you're giving so much that customers cannot help but want to pay your regular prices because of everything you're doing to help them.

Providing incredible value means you're solving the problems your clients have better than anyone else and often leads to you being able to increase your price and charge more than anyone else.

The more value you provide, the more profitable you become.

Think of all the ways you currently help your customers and look for ways to do more.

As an example, at Intersol Digital, we offer bulk sms solutions with higher charges than our competitors and in return we provide them very reliable sms services by being prompt with our timing of messages. We guarantee our clients a wider outreach and because we charge more we take the pains to get phone numbers for our clients, thereby saving them the stress of getting numbers themselves.

It helps cement my company as an expert and does not cost me any extra time or money.

High perceived value + low actual investment = win

Find a Mentor

"Your mentors in life are important, so choose them wisely." Robert Kiyosaki

The fastest and most effective way to grow your business is to model the strategies of people who have already done what you are trying to do.

Success leaves clues and by taking a deeper look into how people you respect became successful, you can take what worked for them, modify it to fit your business.

My first real business was a domain hosting company.

At first it was overwhelming. I was young, I did not know much about internet and hosting, and was not a domain expert either.

I researched domain and hosting companies to see how they got started and we implemented clues from their success into our business. It worked.

First I recommend you look at the big players in your industry and find out their stories. Study them and find out what they did to achieve success?

If you cannot find someone or a company directly related to your industry, then look for one in a similar field.

Secondly look at people you respect even if they are not in your industry and try to model their success

Are you a fan of Donald Trump or Bill Gates? How about Anil Ambani or Michael Adenuga?

✓ **Modeling mentors would definitely get you up there.**

Be Different, Be You

"Whatever you do, be different – that was the advice my mother gave me, and I can't think of better advice for an entrepreneur. If you're different, you will stand out." Anita Roddick

If you are an average company, selling an average product at an average price guess what happens?

Average results (at best).

You need to find a way to stand out.

Been different will improve your chances of securing new jobs and also getting new clients. For example, if someone asks you, what you do?

And you say, I am a website designer, by answering that way you have already scored fewer points, because there are over a million website designers. But if you rather answer by stating that you help companies to have an online presence and passing their message online to more clients. Then you have created a different opinion, a special and different one that will generate more questions.

Create one simple pitch that explains who you help and the benefits they receive.

Use it every time you introduce yourself to someone, even if you do not think they are a potential client.

Think about what makes you different as a person from everyone else? What combined set of interests and experiences can you bring that nobody else knows?
What do you do differently? Help your business stand out by focusing on a niche and injecting your own personality into it.

Do not Spend Until You Earn

> "Innovation has nothing to do with how many R&D dollars you have. When Apple came up with the Mac, IBM was spending at least 100 times more on R&D. It is not about money. It is about the people you have, how you're led, and how much you get it." - Steve Jobs

Anyone can have a million ways to spend a million naira but not everyone can have a single way to make a million naira and that is the difference between successful entrepreneurs and everyone else.

It would have been very easy to start a business if it was just to get an office, print business cards, buy up supplies and inventory and launch a website.

✓ **Turns out that's actually the wrong way to start a business, only spend money when you see that you are making money.**

Instead, spend your time getting to know your customers.
Understand their pain points, offer a solution, and ask if they would pay you for it.

You do not need to spend any money to get your first client but you do need to invest your time and energy.

Once you find a client and have a little bit of money coming then you are ready to spend some money to get more clients. You know the type of person who is going to buy from you and you know how you can help them.

✓ **At the start of any project you are never sure if it will work out.**

You cannot be sure of what will work until you try it.
Start small, invest your time, see what is working, and invest more time and then your money into the projects that are paying off.

Promote on a zero Budget

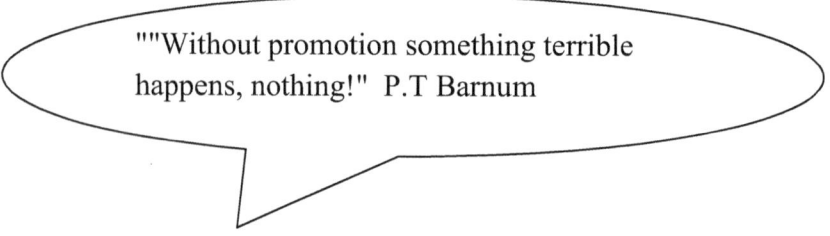

""Without promotion something terrible happens, nothing!" P.T Barnum

If you want to have success as an entrepreneur you better be really good at what you do and be an industry expert.
When reporters are covering stories guess what they always look for?

An expert to comment on it.

Pick up your daily newspaper and read almost any story and you will see that an industry expert is quoted and is sharing their opinions.
Why can't that industry expert be you?
You can start by building your own media list.

This should not be too hard.
Look at the websites of all the trade media who cover your industry and the sections of major media who might run stories about your industry.

Do not be a Quitter

If you are following your life's purpose and are doing meaningful work to help people with your business, the final step to getting past survival is to not quit.

At some point in every entrepreneur's life they think about quitting.

How easy would it be to make a secure salary, get your vacation time every year, and leave your work at work every night so you can spend time with your family and friends.

Most entrepreneurs will go through that period of self-doubt multiple times!

It is important that you don not quit. You will never forgive yourself if you do and you will not bring nearly as much value to this world either.

But if you are really doing something that has meaning and you are having an impact on people then you have to keep going.

You might have to change your business model, find different customers, introduce a new product or service, increase your prices, and restructure your entire company.

- **Do it.**
- **Do not quit.**
- **Just find a different way to stand.**

CHAPTER FOUR

STARTUP TIPS

- ✓ **Honesty**

    Starting up a business will require you to meet and discuss with a lot of people, while striving to get funds, in the process of setting your office, hiring staffs and a lot of other tasks.

    In all these one thing that will determine your business success is honesty. Be honest to a fault, if that could possibly be true. Be honest with yourself and others. Do not tolerate any form of dis honesty

- ✓ **Tell an engaging story**

    It is not the story, it is you, it is how you tell it; you have to tell your story better and better every day. This is the first thing you must learn how to do as a startup business man. As you start your business, customers and clients are listening attentively to what you have to offer, use an engaging story to show them that you have got more than they need.

- ✓ **Build your concept from scratch**

    Creating a new business where none existed before is a very unique skill. Do not worry yourself with how you came by the idea; rather try to build the concept from the very beginning. Use a builder's mentality to build a very good foundation to your concept and business.

- ✓ **Stay motivated all the time**

    I know that this is harder than it sounds; it is like performing two shows a day on stage without pay. Somehow you have to find a way to keep yourself going and that is to stay motivated. Learn how to motivate yourself and staff by being motivated yourself.

Think about the entry

Every product can be designed better: Fact.
Just because you have the best product or idea today, does not mean you will have it tomorrow. Someone will always have a better idea/product, a product that will look better, work faster or cost less. For startup businesses the way to avoid this is to focus more on the entry rather. Think about the barriers to the entry of your product and service and find a way round it.

Worry more about the small competitors

One big distraction when setting up a small business is worrying about the big guys, most times the big guys will completely disregard your idea or overlook your product. The key is focusing on the small competitor in your surroundings.

Think new ways

It does not matter if you are out eating or having a haircut, the startup person should always think of new ways of doing things. Tony Christianson of Cherry Tree Ventures used to have a drawer full of business ideas, actually concepts that needed "starting." Most of the time, the ideas come from impatience or unhappiness about a current product or service.

Keep bad news secret

As a startup person your job is to never give up, once you start engaging in pity parties and telling your workers the bad news then you are doing your job the wrong way. Your people need to believe that no matter what the danger, you are going to lead them to the Promised Land.

Be color blind

One thing you must do as a startup is to never choose one side. At all times you must have an open mind that will make you take only the right decisions that will affect your business positively.

- ✓ **No one cares as much as you do**

    Your new company will consume you and even most of your employees, not even your employees care as much as you do. Always keep in mind that you are the only one who cares that much

- ✓ **Model the behavior you require**

    If you demand certain things, do those things yourself, better to a higher degree. This means getting to work on time, and so forth.

- ✓ **Be accessible and approachable**

    Things happen so fast in the startup that you must simply be there. This means in your office and where people are working.

- ✓ **Put people in positions where they can be successful**

    Get to know your employees and spot their differences. Your job besides being the boss is helping them find success, you must find out what position or tools they need to do the job you are demanding of them.

- ✓ **Find a top sales man**

    It is very important that you either find or nurture a top performing sales person. If you do not have such, high level goals are really hard to achieve. Always keep your eyes out for this sales leader. He will help you in many, many ways.

- ✓ **Customers are not always right**

    Surprised? Customers are not always right, infact some are unreasonable and unprofitable to your business. Realize this fast. Do not misunderstand this to mean that you mistreat customers, far from it. But if a bad customer is negatively impacting you, your top performers and the business in general. Fire them

Dream globally think locally

Sure, it is way fun to think about serving customers in every state and foreign country. You should think about your business in regional or international terms. Just be aware that your best and earliest customers will come from your hometown or where you leave.

Be comfortable being in charge

At the end of the day, in your new developing company, you are it. It makes no difference how complete your team or even how good, or how well you are doing, you are in charge. Everyone looks to you. You need to figure out the key success factor in your business and get all consumed by it.

Just stay in business

Too many companies flame out every day as much as too many people start a company every day. But once it happens, that is it, no more power; you have lost your business; if you can just continue your business, first year to second year and to the third. Chances are great that you will make it to the happy years. Do whatever it takes just to stay in business.

Your sales people do not work for you

The sooner you realize that all good sales people work truly for the customers and not for you, you will understand more about sales people than 90% of all non-sales people.

Be an active good listener

Soon you will be a boss; everyone would want to give you ideas and advices on how to improve your already successful business. Your job is to develop an attentive ear, some of the advices might actually help propel your business and besides the business part. You would learn a lot just by listening to people.

CHAPTER FIVE

A GREAT TIME FOR STARTUPS
Why you should start now

There has never been a better time to start a business. After reading this book you should make starting your own business a top priority. It is time to start a business and be your own boss. This is your opportunity to join the ever increasing world of self-employed people.

Adults and young ones are gradually turning their talent into a way of making a living whilst experienced professionals are opting for the freedom and flexibility that comes with self-employment.

This has nothing to do with age, color or gender.
There is potential to turn a passion or skill into a bright business idea.

- ✓ *Low start-up costs*

You can start almost any kind of business from your smartphone, business cards and at most a budget of at most five figures. You can now start a business with a greater ease, make sales and set up operations with ease and from home.

- ✓ *Technology*

The world is changing. Technology is defining the way we leave our lives. Computers and smartphones are the order of the day. It is now easier than ever to start a business than it was in the past because of this new technology. Social media platforms and trading sites offer start-ups a powerful route to market. Selling and promoting yourself online is more affordable and achievable and successful businesses are being built on Facebook and promoted via Twitter, YouTube and LinkedIn, selling everything from clothings to Softwares, even fairly used products.

- ✓ *High level of support*

If you are starting a business today, you won't be alone!
There is an abundance of support to help you start and grow.

At the very early stages of your startup, you can always raise finance from relatives, colleagues, governments, banks and a lot of other institutions designed to assist start-up.

The startup phase in business is arguably the hardest phase; you have to question and answer yourself. Seeking answers to problem that may come up later.

One of these questions is asking yourself how good your idea is. Is the idea a good business proposition? Is there a market and demand for you to make sales and make a profit? Think about the cost and time elements of the business.

You do not necessarily need to know all the answers to your questions immediately; you can make a plan while working on answering the questions correctly.
Use good, resourceful business guidance and support to help bring your business idea to the fore front.

Make a plan. Write a business plan that acts as your route map. Good business plans are simple and clear, they address key areas like: Background on you, your team and its capabilities, your business idea and a description of your product/service, costs, pricing and sales forecast.

Make noise. Get to know the media that covers your industry and send them good stories with top quality images. Make the most of social media to become known as an expert in your field and as free marketing.

Make sales. Target friends and family as customers and branch out from there. Price your product at a rate that is competitive and covers the cost of your time. Make sales at events and through local shops.

Keep the business in balance

Try to spend quality time strategizing on how to develop your business to the next level. Think of innovative and creative ways to give your business the needed push. That way, both you and the business will stay in productive and profitable balance.

Your home may offer you your biggest business resource when starting a business especially with low funds. So you do not have to worry much if you cannot raise enough finance to rent an office space. You can setup a home office and once you make enough money you move out. Take advantage of reduced costs, no commute and the flexibility that comes with building a business around the family.

Helping hands

Large corporates and other businesses are actively seeking to support small businesses in a range of ways.

Like offers of space, mentoring and access to customers and capital, because they recognize that firms like yours can be customers for them in the future and the products and services you offer could be solutions to their business needs.

Brands like Microsoft and Google are running competitions and offering their services and support entrepreneurs and small start-ups.

Why not search the websites of corporate firms that buy or supply products and services related to your business and see how they might work with a small firm like you?

Improve and grow

You are up and running and your focus has been to build up sales, keep in profit and do well it is time for you to start planning how to develop the business and build for future growth.

Here is what International Business Machine (IBM) has to tell you about midsize business.

The world is changing. Midsize businesses are leading the way.

We are living on a very different planet from the one we lived on even a few years ago. The age of the globally integrated economy and society has arrived. The world is becoming flatter which means any sized business, from any place on earth, can now establish a global footprint. In fact, midsize and small businesses alone are now responsible for nearly 65% of the global GDP. As our planet becomes smarter, midsize businesses will wield more of the influence that once belonged to only the largest enterprises. IBM and our Business Partners are providing the support and know-how to help turn their vision into reality and their ideas into results. Midsize businesses are the engines of a Smarter Planet. Let's build a smarter planet. IBM

CHAPTER SIX

MAKING YOUR BUSINESS PLAN YOUR ONLY PLAN

Plan to succeed

Have you ever wondered why ninety percent of startup businesses wind up before the end of one financial year? Well, there are a lot of reasons why they do. One reason is not having a business plan before start up.

To prepare a business plan, one must think through its business in detail and set objectives. Preparation of a business plan will enable benchmarks to be set against which the business's future performance can be monitored.

Preparing a business plan will also highlight the resources needed to achieve its plans.

What is a business plan?

A business plan is basically a document which:
- ✓ **Sets out individual/company's plans**
- ✓ **Shows how those plans can be achieved and**
- ✓ **Demonstrates that the planned outcome meets the requirements of the reader**

The business plan should describe you, your company and project concisely and accurately. However, a business plan is also a selling document and the description should therefore also be attractive.

There are two main purposes for writing a business plan. The first and most important is to serve as a guide during the life of your business, the blueprint of your business and will serve to keep you on the right track. Second, the business plan is a requirement if you are planning to seek loan funds, it will provide potential lenders with detailed information on all aspects of the company's past and current operations and provide future projections.

Who? What? Where? When? Why? How? How Much?

Answer all of the questions asked by the key words in one paragraph at the beginning of each section of the business plan. Then expand on that statement by telling more about each item in the text that follows.

Cover sheet

The first page of your business plan will be the cover sheet. It serves as the title page of your plan. It should contain the following information:

Name of the company
Company address
Company phone number
Logo (if you have one)
Names, titles, addresses, phone numbers of owners
Month and year in which the plan is issued
Name of preparer

Statement of purpose (Mission Statement)

The statement of purpose is also called the mission statement or executive summary. It should be concise and clear. The statement of purpose is contained on one page. Although positioned after the cover sheet, it is most effectively written after the plan has been completed.

The business

The first major section of your plan covers the details of your business. Begin this section with a one-page summary addressing the key elements of your business. Address all of the topics as they relate to your business in an order that seems logical to you. Include information about your industry in general, and your business in particular. Be prepared to back up statements and justify projections with data.

Legal Structure

State the reasons for your choice of legal structure. If you are a sole proprietor, you may include a copy of your business license. It must spell out the distribution of profits and financial responsibility for any losses if you are in a partnership.

Description of the Business

This is the section of the plan in which you go into greater detail about your business. Answer the key word questions regarding the business's history and present status and your future projections for research and development.

Outline your current business assets and report your inventory in terms of size, value, rate of turnover and marketability. Include industry trends, stress the uniqueness of your product or service and state how you can benefit your customers.

Products or Services

Give a detailed description of your product, from raw materials to finished item. What raw materials are used, how much do they cost, who are your suppliers, where are they located and why did you choose them? Include cost breakdowns and rate sheets to back up your statements.

If you are providing a service, tell what your service is, how you are able to provide it, how it is provided, who will be doing the work and where the service will be performed. Tell why your business is unique and what you have that is special to your customers. If you have both a product and a service that work together to benefit your customers be sure to mention this in your plan. Again the key words come into use.

You should state any proprietary rights, such as copyrights, patents or trademarks, in this section.

Location

If location is important to your marketing plan, you may focus on it in the marketing section.

Management

This section describes who is behind the business. If you are a sole proprietor, tell about your abilities and include your resume. Be honest about areas in which you will need help and state how you will get that help. Will you take a marketing seminar, work with an accountant or seek the advice of someone in advertising?

If you have formed a partnership, explain why the partners were chosen, what they bring to the company and how their abilities complement each other's.

Personnel

Who will be doing the work? Why are they qualified? How will they be hired? What is their wage? What will they be doing? Outline the duties and job descriptions for all personnel. Explain any employee benefits.

Summary

You have now covered all the areas which should be addressed in the business section. Use the key words, be thorough, anticipate any problem areas and be prepared with solutions. Be ready to project your business into the future, when you have completed the business section, you are ready to begin developing the marketing section.

Marketing

The second major section of your business plan covers the details of your marketing plan. A good marketing plan is essential to your business development and success. Include information about the total market with emphasis on your target market. You must take the time to identify your customers and find the means to make your product or service available to them. The key here is time. It takes time to research and develop a marketing plan, but it is time well spent.

Begin this section with a one-page summary covering the key elements of your marketing plan.

Target Market

The target market has been defined as that group of customers with a set of common characteristics that distinguish them from other customers. You want to identify that set of common characteristics that will make those customers yours. Tell how you did your market research. What were your resources and your results? What are the demographics of your target market? Where do your customers live, work and shop? Do they shop where they live or where they work?

Competition

Direct competition is a company offering the same product or service to the same market. Indirect competition is a company with the same product or service but with a different target market. Evaluate both types of competitors. You want to determine the competitors' images. To what part of the market are they trying to appeal? Can you appeal to the same market in a better way? Or can you find an untapped market?

Methods of Distribution

Distribution is the manner in which products are physically transported to the consumer or the way services are made available to the customer. Distribution is closely related to your target market.

Advertising

Advertising presents the message to your customer that your product or service is good and desirable. Tailor your advertising to your target market.

Pricing

Your pricing structure is critical to the success of your business and is determined through market research and analysis of financial considerations. Basic marketing strategy is to price within the range between the price ceiling and the price floor. The price ceiling is determined by the market; the highest cost a consumer will pay for a product or service and is based on perceived value. What is the competition charging? What is the quality of the product or service you are offering? What is the nature of the demand and what is the image you are projecting? The price floor is the lowest amount at which you can offer a product or service, meet all your costs and still make your desired profit. Consider all costs, raw materials, office overhead, shipping, taxes, loans and interest payments. The profitable business operates between the price ceiling and the price floor. The difference allows for discounts, bad debt and returns. Be specific about how you arrived at your pricing structure and leave room for some flexibility.

Product Design

Packaging and product design can play a major role in the success of your business. It is what first catches the customer's eye. Consider the tastes of your target market in the ultimate design of your product and your package design. Decide what will be most appealing in terms of size, shape, color, material and wording. Packaging attracts a great deal of public attention.

Timing of Market Entry

The timing of your entry into the marketplace is critical and takes careful planning and research. Having your products and services available at the right time and the right place depends more on understanding consumer readiness than on your organizational schedule. The manner in which a new product is received by the consumer can be affected by the season, the weather and holidays.

Industry Trends

Be alert for changes in your industry. New technology may bring new products into the marketplace that will generate new service businesses. Read trade journals and industry reports in your field. Project how your market may change and what you plan to do to keep up.

Financial Documents

You are now ready to develop the third area of your plan. Financial records are used to show past, current and projected finances. In this section we will cover the major documents you will need to include in your business plan.

Summary of Financial Needs

If you are applying for a loan, your lenders and investors will analyze the needs of your business. This document is an outline telling why you are applying for a loan and how much you need.

Cash Flow Statement (Budget)

Cash flow statements are the documents that project what your business plan means in terms of money. They show cash inflow and outflow over a period of time and are used for internal planning. If you have been in business for some time, worksheets can be put together from the actual figures of income and expenses of previous years combined with projected changes for the next period. If you are starting a new business, you will have to project your financial needs and disbursements. Your profit at the end of the year will depend on the proper balance between cash inflow and outflow. The cash flow statement identifies

When cash is expected to be received.

How much cash will be received

When cash must be spent to pay bills and debts.

How much cash will be needed to pay expenses.

It also allows the manager to identify the source of necessary cash, i.e. will it come from sales and services rendered or must it be borrowed? Be sure that your projections take into account receivables and how long it will take your customer to pay. The cash flow statement deals only with actual cash transactions and not with depreciation.

A cash flow statement can be prepared for any period of time. It is recommended that you match the fiscal year of your business. It should be prepared on a monthly basis for the next year and revised not less than quarterly to reflect actual performance in the preceding three months of operations.

Completing Your Cash Flow Statement

The vertical columns of a cash flow statement represent the twelve months, preceded by a total column. Horizontal rows on the statement contain figures for the sources of cash and cash to be paid out.

Break-even Analysis

The break-even point is the point at which a company's expenses exactly match its sales or service volume; The point at which the business will neither make a profit nor incur a loss. The break-even point can be calculated in either mathematical or graphical form. It can be expressed in total naira or revenue exactly offset by total expenses or in total units of production (cost of which equals exactly the income derived by sales).

To apply a break-even analysis to a business operation, two types of expenses must first be projected: fixed costs and variable costs. Fixed costs do not vary with sales or output. Variable costs vary in direct proportion to the output; the greater the volume of sales, the higher the cost.

The *balance sheet*

This is a financial statement, usually prepared at the close of an accounting period that shows the financial position of the business as of a fixed date; A picture of your firm's financial condition at a particular moment. By regularly preparing this statement, you will be able to identify and analyze trends in the financial strength of your business and thus implement timely modifications.

Income Statement

The income (profit and loss) statement shows your business financial activity over a period of time, usually your tax year. In contrast to the balance sheet, which shows a picture of your business at a given moment, this statement can be likened to a moving picture. It shows what has happened in your business over a period of time. The income statement is an excellent tool for assessing your business. You will be able to pick out weaknesses in your operation and plan ways to run your business more effectively and thereby increase your profits.

Development

The income statement shows where your money has come from and where it was spent over a specific period of time. It should be prepared not only at the end of the fiscal year, but at the close of each business month.

Supporting Documents

Now that you have completed the main body of your business plan, you will need to include a separate section for any additional records that should be included to support your plan. Supporting documents are the records that back up the statements and decisions made in the three main parts of your plan.

Keeping your business plan current

If your business plan is going to be effective either to the business or to a potential lender, it will be necessary for you to update it on a regular basis. Changes necessitating revisions can be attributed to three sources: changes within the company, changes originating with the customer and technological changes. Neglecting to allow for these changes will doom your operation to decreased profits and probable failure.

Implementing Changes

As the owner, you must be aware of changes in your industry, market and community. First you must determine what revisions are needed. You will have to compare your plan with the changes discussed above. You can use your employees to help keep track of business trends applicable to their expertise. However, the final judgment as to revisions will rest with you, the owner. You may make errors, but with experience, your percentage of correct decisions will increase and your reward will be higher profits.

CHAPTER SEVEN

FINANCIAL MANAGEMENT

> Good financial management is critical to the success of any business. Without it, a business can be set for failure from the start

✓ **It is not lack of customers or products that will destroy a business – it is lack of cash.**

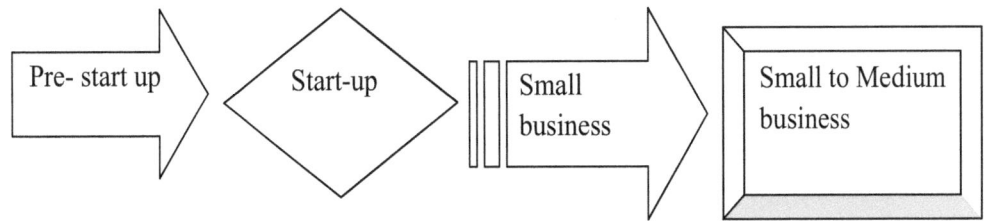

The four stages of business development

There are **four key stages** in the development of a start-up. At each stage, a business owner will need to consider an element of financial management which will help their business stay healthy and achieve its potential.

Pre start-up

This can be the most critical stage in the success of a business idea.

❖ Researching the market and assessing potential demand for your product or service should be undertaken now.

❖ Each business should produce a business plan incorporating financial forecasts.

Key questions

✓ Have you developed a business plan and financial forecasts?

- ✓ Have you spoken to a qualified professional business advisor when developing your business and financial forecasts? (E.g. accountant, lawyer, bank manager)
- ✓ Is your business plan backed up by a marketing and product development plan?

Start-up

Taking into account financial forecasts, this is the stage where a business plan is implemented.

- ❖ Cash management is critical at this stage.
- ❖ Small businesses fail when they run out of cash.
- ❖ This is the stage where business owners will consider securing finance to grow their business, strong financial management is vital for a good credit rating.

Key questions

- ✓ How do you manage your day-to-day cash flow?
- ✓ Have you developed a management plan?
- ✓ How do you monitor performance and keep business costs to a minimum?

Small business

This is the stage where the business has overcome the start-up stage.

- ❖ A small business should seek qualified independent financial advice before accessing finance to grow their business. Audit, assurance and management accounting will be helpful.

Key questions

- ✓ What is the next stage for your business? Does your business plan and financial forecasts reflect the next phase of company growth?
- ✓ Does the business have enough finance to meet its needs? Is accessing finance a problem? If so, what are you doing to address this?
- ✓ Do you produce regular management accounts?

Small to medium-sized business

This is the stage where a small business may grow in size. As a result, they will have a wide group of stakeholders who often require audit and assurance of their business' finances.

- Some small businesses may consider accessing a wider range of finance

Key questions

- Is your finance team managed by a professionally qualified accountant?
- Does the Board regularly review the risks the business faces
- Are budget and cash flow projections produced and discussed by the management team?
- Are monthly management accounts produced in time to be useful in assessing the performance of the business?
- Do you hold regular meetings with finance providers to review business plans and financing options?

CHAPTER EIGHT

INNOVATION
Thinking ahead of competition

"If you can't compete on price you have to differentiate, and to differentiate you have to innovate!" Andy Bruce,

Innovation is the application of new ideas to products, processes, and other aspects of the activities of a company that leads to increased "value."

A product innovation means bringing a new product that improves the range and quality of products on offer: for example, the Apple iPod is an innovation compared with the Sony Walkman, which was an earlier portable device for playing music.

Innovating for competitive edge

Innovation is a core business proficiency of the 21st century, in order to not only compete and grow but to survive in a global economy, businesses must innovate.

Innovation is a key aspect of business. There is absolutely no room in today's market for companies and individuals that cannot continually envision and bring innovation to the market.

Innovation is critical if you must succeed in today's business world. There is more need to deliver higher value for products and services in order to beat competition. Workers, services, products and infrastructure must be innovative enough to produce high profit results that will enable business to compete and win.

Why innovation is necessary

Starting a business or managing an existing business can be a very difficult task especially without innovation; before now business won competitions solely on pricing but those times are far gone.

Today people will only patronize your product when they know it suits their future needs.

How do you provide services and sell products that add value to your customers?

The way forward is innovation. As a business man you have to think ahead of your customers, you have to get into their heads early enough to know what they would prefer in the future; the kind of products and services that would be appeal to them years from now.

Come up with innovative ideas, know how to execute them and you will be further and further ahead of your competitors.

What is holding you back?

Whenever the concept of innovation is discussed in a business context it is often misunderstood.

So what really is innovation in a business context?

First of all innovation should not be restricted to:

Ground-breaking ideas and discoveries or technological leap forwards
Creativity 'workshops'
Product based companies
Hi-tech companies

Innovation is not about big discoveries and giant changes to businesses. Innovation is often about minor, incremental changes to products, services and processes.

It includes all players in every industry. It includes all workers in every department. From Public Relations department, Audit, Customer care to Finance department. It needs to be well managed and planned. It has to be treated as an important business process that cannot be done without.

It has to be integrated into the business at every level in order to succeed in the 21st business century.

For your product to stand out and for it to have a good customer following, Innovation must be well utilized as a skill and process.

- ✓ Innovation should be managed as efficiently as all the other business process.
- ✓ Successful innovation companies operate an 'Innovation Hub' where all ideas and innovations are collated and coordinated.

Ideas must be effectively selected, bad ideas killed off. This process helps to prevent innovation overload. It avoids the situation where a company is almost paralyzed by the volume of ideas and innovation gotten from the process of innovation

If new ideas and innovation will make a difference, there are certain criteria that they must satisfy.

Value – does the idea deliver tangible benefits to the organization? These questions help eliminate those ideas and innovations that are good in principle but add little or no value to the bottom line, now or in the future.

Suitable – is it consistent with strategy and the current situation? This helps eliminate those ideas that are potential distractions and move the business needlessly away from its core business focus.

Acceptable – will all stakeholders support it? Often innovations fail in large companies because of the 'not invented here' syndrome. It is crucial that proponents of an idea or innovation spend time and effort on selling the idea internally and gauging the level of support for it.

Feasible – are there sufficient resources and time? Can the innovation be managed within existing budgets or will additional funding be required? Do new skills need to be acquired to implement this idea effectively?

Enduring – will the idea deliver value in both the long and short term? If a new idea or innovation is to be truly strategic will it survive the rigors of time? Is the long term gain worth the short term pain of bringing a new idea to market?

The innovation train

One feature of successful businesses is the 'Innovation Train' generating unlimited ideas to propel a product forward into the future.

The innovation train is missing from most companies. The innovation train is a process that helps in the development of a product, whether a new or existing product. In the process products are examined, re-produced and incremental improvements are made on the products. Ideas are also generated, ideas that will hold off competition.

There has to be an innovation system designed to improve products, services and attain competitive edge. It involves all departments in a company.

It includes brainstorming sessions with marketing, product development and management to help find new ideas that will excite customers; a process that help companies to choose the next right direction in order to create competitive advantage.

Providing high value for customers can only be attained through this process, most times all business or a product needs is a minor shift in the approach to the future.

Companies need to be able to predict the future, and predict correctly in order to be a people to people based company.

So then what exactly is an innovation train?

The innovation train is the value that management of a company places on innovation. How much importance is innovation to the company? Once a company values innovation and puts into practice the tools of innovation, the process of innovation and undergoes innovation trainings then the company is building their 'innovation train'.

The innovation process

✓ Innovation should be built into business routines whether 'passive' or 'reactive',

A culture of innovation should be created where day to day activities and management seek to enable innovations to flourish.

The most important element of the innovation train is the plan put in place by the management of a company to move the company towards innovation.

Innovation life cycle

- Ideation: The creative process of generating, developing, and communicating new ideas. In this phase an idea is understood. The ideas are aimed at improving a service or a product.

- Concept development: The process of improving and developing new concepts before committing extensive resources. The concept has to be developed up to what is required. Once certain that the concept is what is needed then it can now undergo the next phase.

- Evaluation; The process of using quantitative and qualitative methods to evaluate concepts. Evaluating concepts to determine how the concept is going to serve in a longer term.

- Commercialization: The process that converts ideas and research into viable products and services that retains the desired functionality. When ideation happens and the concept is developed and evaluated, the next step is turning the ideas and concepts into a product or a service.

- Incremental innovation (improvement) the final phase of the innovation lifecycle process has to do with the series of small changes and improvements made to a product or a service that usually helps a company to maintain or improve its competitive position over time

The innovation life cycle process has to be organized in such a way that engages all departments and everyone in the company. As much as there are numerous rewards in involving everyone in the innovation life cycle process, it also has to be well managed in order to avoid distraction to everyday working.

Tools for innovation

Tools for innovation are basically things that can help in innovation. Most of the very important tools relate to the early stages of the innovation life cycle process.

The ideas that are needed to begin to begin a successful innovation lifecycle. The first part of innovation lifecycle is the "ideation phase" where the ideas and concepts of innovation are formed. It is much more than brainstorming sessions, one of its main functions is to provide direction to the innovation team.

The ideation process must bring together persons that have been trained and prepared for the innovation process.

Building your innovation train

Nothing has more impact on a company than the preparation for success.

One way of being prepared is to build an innovation train.

First, most people learn best when they get the chance to experience something new rather than being told. This is one effect innovation training has on the innovation process.

Also the skill of learning something new and then applying it in practical ways will not only improve the old capability but also create a value.

The need to build an innovation train is a must in today's business world. It is not good for a company to start innovating when competition becomes stronger; doing that will only lead to failure in the long run as it would be too late, rather early innovation will create the need to constantly generate competitive advantage.

The value of preparing yourself and your people to innovate will pay dividends beyond the new product and services. It will also help everyone to innovate on better ways to do their jobs.

An innovation train is what you need if you want your product to excel. You can start building yours today and experience the impact of innovation on your business.

CHAPTER NINE

PEOPLE WANT BRANDS

Making the brand the strategic 'driver' for the entire organization

> "Products are made in the factory, but brands are created in the mind" Walter Landor

The concept of "brand" is one of the most misunderstood terms in today's business lexicon.

Let's start by going over the following questions

*1. Which is **a known** corporate brand?*
a. Sony
b. Coca Cola
c. Microsoft
d. HP
e. All of the above

2. What is a brand...?
a. a logo?
b. a jingle?
c. a tagline?
d. a product?
e. a positioning?
f. none of the above?

The answer to the first question is "all of the above". Yes, they are all influential names in the business world. Sony, Coca Cola, HP and Microsoft are all known corporate brands.

Their corporate names are linked with such quality products such as Softwares, Televisions, Beverages and consumer electronics like Computers and computing devices. And for the second question, if you answered "none of the above" then you were totally right.

A logo, jingle, tagline, product or positioning are all representations of the brand or a means to promote what the brand stands for. But they are not the brand

What exactly is a brand?

A brand is neither a logo nor a slogan, an identity nor a symbol, a brand is the feeling or experience a customer has with a company's products and services

A brand is all of the promises, assurances and perceptions that an organization wants its customers to feel about its products and services. The image a company creates about its products and services to the customers.

If you device a means to tell your customers how good your product is, why they should buy your product and how useful your product will be to them, then there is every possibility that when they see your products on the store shelves they will not only buy it but will also have the conviction to buy any product that comes from the brand.

For example we all like Sony products because we feel it is superior and unique in terms of production. That single assumption and assurance covers every product Sony produces be it new or old.

The brand is as important to an organization as its people, equipment and capital, at such it has to be nurtured with attention, care and investment. Strategic branding goes far beyond marketing activities. The face of the business strategy is reflected in the brand-customer relationship.

Most people think of branding as the visible items seen by everyone at the store shelves, but really the valuable aspects of branding are often only seen internally, or below the water.

When a company has a strong brand it means that it has avoided some wrong turns. They also escape duplication of product.

It also keeps everyone on the course because they have a shared vision, they know where they want to take the company to and the kind of experience they wish customers and clients to have using their products and services.

Branding also serves as an advantage in the process of hiring staffs and accepting new clients. It reduces the mistakes made by companies in this process because you easily know who is fit or not for the job. This aspect alone saves companies huge amount of money on a yearly basis.

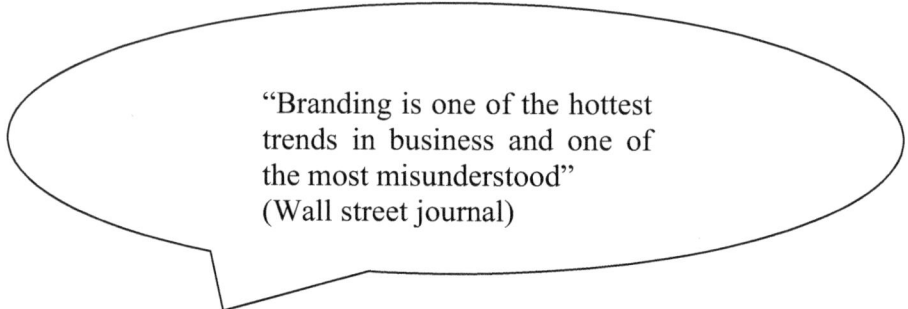

"Branding is one of the hottest trends in business and one of the most misunderstood" (Wall street journal)

Why most companies do not do branding?

You might want to ask me why everyone does not have a strong brand if it has so many advantages.

The answer is this

- ✓ Branding requires a lot of discipline.
- ✓ Branding is not an instant solution. It requires people, time, resources and investment to make it succeed
- ✓ Branding goes beyond marketing. It involves every department in a company
- ✓ Branding means always staying true to your word: so at all times the company has to provide service and produce products that will reflect positively on its brands
- ✓ Branding means you cannot be everything to everyone.

Bottom line is branding requires hard work but the gains are definitely worth the investment.

The keys to successful branding

Now that you know what branding is, it is time for you to know the key to having a successful brand.

- ✓ It is about **you,**

It has to do with you, you need to have a different mindset about your business and what it has to do to win and keep customers.

It is about understanding that a brand is not just about a customer's head but his heart too.

It is about knowing that a brand is not just an activity but knowing what your brand is about, and that is a good experience for the customer.

It is about looking out of the box as a customer rather than looking in as business owner.

The second is influence. Influence your customer's experience of your business. If you must build a successful brand then you must understand that you have to build influence. The good news is that it is not a Titanic boat so it is achievable.

The way to having an influence over your customers' perception of your brand is by creating what James Hammond calls a 'Brand Halo'.

It consists of the following components mentioned earlier like: logos, mission statements, slogans and the like.

Unlike using these elements independently this time they will be part of an overall dialogue with the customer that only stops when you can no longer be bothered to have something to say.

A brand halo displays what a company has to offer in the best possible light. If presented correctly, you will have a strong brand. It does not matter what kind of business you are into, any manufacturer or service provider can build a strong brand.

Building your brand halo

You can build your brand halo with the following word 'EPIC'

E- Stands for Emotion. The key part of creating your powerful brand and on it everything else will be built. Without emotion in your product and service, you do not have a brand but commodity rather.

P- Stands for Perception. Emotions are stirred by sensory stimulation that arrives at the brain through five senses: sight, sound, smell, taste and touch.

Using all five senses in the process will enable you to really build a strong perception of the brand in the customers' mind.

I-stands for INNOVATION. Being aware of the five senses is one thing. Innovation is what keeps the business brand alive and kicking. It provides the brand the power to carry on for years, it also provides the freshness needed to keep your brand on top.

C- Stands for Communication. Why do you want to create an emotional brand? What is your purpose and why should customers care? Use narratives to communicate to your audience, your business, along with your aims and achievements.

CHAPTER TEN

FORMAL EXPRESSIONS IN BUSINESS

These are phrases and sentences that will help you speak Business English more effectively.

How to introduce yourself formally

I'd like to introduce myself
I'd like to introduce myself. I'm Oru Russell from Bayelsa.

Let me introduce myself
Let me introduce myself. Mr. Oru Russell.

My name is
My name is Oru Russell.

How to reply to a formal introduction

Nice to meet you
Nice to meet you, Hon. Jackson

Pleased to meet you.
Pleased to meet you, Jackson. I'm Engr. Larry

How to introduce yourself before a speech

I am
I am Dr. Favour from Bayelsa.

I'd like to introduce myself
I'd like to introduce myself. I am Oru Favour, Public Relations officer.

Let me introduce myself
Let me introduce myself. Oru Favour.

How to Introduce people to the public

This is
This is Kind Dickson.

May I introduce?
May I introduce Kind Dickson? He's our maintenance guy.

I'd like you to meet
I'd like you to meet Kind Dickson. He's in charge of our maintenance team.

✓ **How to say Hello**

Hi
  Hi, Mabel.

Hello
Hello. May I come in?

How are you?
How are you, Mabel?

Good morning
Good morning, Miss Mabel

Nice to see you
Nice to see you again, Mabel

✓ **How to start a meeting**

Let's get started.
Let's get the meetings started. Joshua, would you like to begin?

We need to discuss
We need to discuss about this company.

What brings us here?
What brings us here today? What we need to be a better company.

✓ **How to explain your purpose**

The reason
The reason we are here is to discuss some pending problems.

My aim
My aim is to take this company back to its rightful position.

What I'd like
What I'd like to do is to make some slight changes.

My objective
My objective is to maintain order here.

How to present data orderly

firstly	Secondly	To end
To start with	Then	To conclude
initially	Next	finally
In first place	Following on from	To finish
Let us begin by	After	Last but not the least

Firstly, secondly and to end
Firstly we'll tackle costs; secondly we'll view the balance sheet and to end we'll discuss this year's sales.

To start with, then and to conclude
Kristy will start with the lecture. Then she will answer questions and, to conclude, he will give a test.

How to ask for information

Could you please?
Could you please show me the route?

Would you mind?
Would you mind showing me the route?

I wonder if you could.
I wonder if you could show me the route.

What do you know about?
What do you know about Kristy?

How to ask for further details

Could you add?
Could you add more details to the second point, please?

Could you give us further details?
Could you give us further details on this scheme?

What else?
What else can you add to convince us better?

✓ **How to contact**

Could I contact you?
Could I contact you later on?

How do I get in touch with you?
How do I get in touch with you?

What's your?
What"s your e-mail?

Could I have your?
Could I have you office address please?

✓ **How to emphasize on a point**

This is a key issue
Business relations are a key issue now.

I'd like to emphasise on
I"d like to emphasise on point three of my presentation.

This is vital
Turning a profit this year is vital if we wish to survive.

✓ **How to give instructions**

Before beginning
Before beginning let us check the lights.

I would start by
I would start by going through the report.

We'll set off
We'll set off by going through the report.

To begin with
To begin with, write a business plan.

How to add further information

In addition
In addition, I'd like to mention that Janet is generally right.

As well
Smartphones, as well as laptops, are produced in Nigeria.

Furthermore
Furthermore, they insisted we should join them.

Moreover
Moreover, the fine must be paid within seven days.

How to provide more detail

To elaborate
To elaborate on what Miss Janet exposed we will use a chart.

Here I have further information
Here I have further information. As you see, the weather has changed.

Let me tell you a little more
Let me tell you a bit more about Joecasta and Efosa. they're very reliable.

How to sell a product

It will help you
This book will help you speak better English.

It will improve
Our company will help improve your sales.

The benefits are
The benefits to the company are twofold: lower cost and better yield.

It will allow you
Our cleaning service will allow you to have every morning to yourself.

It stands out
The Clickcee website stands out among its competitors because it is more reliable

22. How to propose what is needed

You might need
You might need an architect to sign the blueprints.

It would be a good idea
It would be a good idea to take a couple of spare computer parts.

It might be better
It might be better to include a color photograph along with the letter.

✓ **How to describe a product**

Let me tell you about
Let me tell you about our latest website.

Can I tell you?
Can I tell you about our school's services? We teach French.

✓ **How to describe the features of a product**

made of
made of wood and aluminum.

It features
The team features two Nobel Prize winners.

It comes with
It comes with a calculator and a pocket translator.

It measures
It measures ten feet in width, two in height and one in depth.

It weighs
It weighs close to a ton.

✓ **How to summarize**

To sum up
To sum up, we are in a very healthy financial situation.

The conclusion is
The conclusion is that all our efforts have finally proven successful.

In a few words
In a few words, Russell would like to congratulate you all.

It all boils down
It all boils down to simple truth: money brings money.

✓ **How to say thanks**

Thanks
Thanks for everything.

Thank you
Thank you for reading this book.

If you found this book helpful

- ✓ Share it with a friend or colleague

- ➢ If you know someone else who might find this book helpful, feel free to recommend it to them.

Subscribe to the Zero to Zillions blog

- ✓ I write the Zero to Zillions blog to share tips on startups and other related topics found in this book. a way of continuously spreading the message. Of course it is free

Mail us at zerotozillions@yahoo.com

Send us your questions, and we shall answer you. Whatever the problem, as long as it has to do with the contents of this book, you can seek our help and be sure we will.
We shall help you achieve your dreams

Also call us on
+2348158681833 for queries and complaints
www.zerotozillions.com

FURTHER READING

Punie, Y., Cabrera, M., Bogdanowicz, M., Zinnbauer, D. & Navajas, E. (2006a). The Future of ICT and Learning in the Knowledge Society, Report on a Joint DG JRC-DG EAC Workshop held in Seville, 20-21 October 2005, EUR 22218 EN.

Covey, S 1990, *The Seven Habits of Highly Effective People*, Simon & Shuster, New York.

Aaker, D.A. (1996), *Building Strong Brands*, The Free Press, New York, NY.

Balmer, J.M.T. (1995), ªCorporate branding and connoisseurshipº, *Journal of General Management*, Vol. 21 No. 1.

Dowling, G.R. (1993), ªDeveloping your company image into a corporate assetº, *Long Range Planning*, Vol. 26 No. 2, pp. 101-9.

Kapferer, J.N. (1992), *Strategic Brand Management*, Kogan Page, London.

Checkland, P. (1987) *Systems Thinking, Systems Practice*.

Floridi, L. (2007) 'A look into the future impact of ICT on our lives', *Information Society* **23**(1): 59–64.

Clifford, Denis, and Ralph Warner. *The Partnership Book*. Berkeley: Nolo Press, 1989.

Goldstein, Harvey. *Up Your Cash Flow*. Los Angeles: Granville Publications, 1986.

Husch, Tony, and Linda Foust. *That's a Great Idea*. Oakland, CA: Gravity Press, 1986.

Levinson, Jay Conrad. *Guerilla Marketing: Secrets for Making Big Profits from Your Small Business*. Boston: Houghton-Mifflin, 1984.

Ogilvy, David. *Ogilvy on Advertising*. New York: Vintage Books, 1985.

Pinson, Linda, and Jerry Jinnett. *Anatomy of a Business Plan*. Tustin, CA: Out of Your Mind...and Into the Marketplace, 1989.

Pinson, Linda, and Jerry Jinnett. *Marketing: Researching*

Geroski, P. 1995. Markets for technology: knowledge, innovation and appropriability. In *Handbook of the Economics of Innovation and Technical Change* (ed.

OECD. 1997. *The Oslo Manual: Proposed Guidelines for Collecting and Interpreting Technological Innovation Data*. Paris: Organisation for Economic

Cooperation and Development. Cachia, R. (2008). Social Computing: The Case of Social Networking.

www.ingramcontent.com/pod-product-compliance
Lightning Source LLC
Chambersburg PA
CBHW040843180526
45159CB00001B/297